A Map of Your State

Use the map of the United States on pages R18–R19 of your social studies textbook to make a map of your own state.

Copy or trace the shape of your state onto a sheet of paper. Locate and label your state capital. Then add a compass rose. Color your map and give it a title. The title of your map could be the name of your state.

McGraw-Hill School Division

GEO ADVENTURE 2

Mystery State in the West

Look at the map of the United States on pages R18–R19 of your social studies textbook. Use these clues to find the mystery state:

    The northwestern border of this state touches Utah. The capital of this state is almost 300 miles North of Santa Fe, New Mexico.

Write the name of the mystery state on a sheet of paper. Then make up clues for your own mystery state. Be sure to use direction words and distances in your clues.

McGraw-Hill School Division

A Nation Grows

Travel to Richmond

GEO ADVENTURE 3

Look at the map of the United States on pages R18–R19 of your social studies textbook.

Suppose you and your family want to take a trip from your state capital to Richmond, Virginia. Which states would you pass through along the way? List the states in order on a sheet of paper. Next to each state write the name of its capital.

McGraw-Hill School Division

A Nation Grows

Find these Cities

Use the map of the United States on pages R18–R19 of your social studies textbook to find the following cities:
- Denver, Colorado
- Austin, Texas
- Pittsburgh, Pennsylvania

List the cities on a sheet of paper. Next to each city write the numbers of the lines of latitude and longitude that are closest to that city.

McGraw-Hill School Division

A Nation Grows

GEO ADVENTURE 5

Which Country?

Use the world map on pages R24–R25 of your social studies textbook to find the mystery country. Here are the clues:

I am a country located in Africa.

I have borders on the Atlantic Ocean and Indian Ocean. I am located at the southern tip of the continent. Which country am I?

McGraw-Hill School Division

GEO ADVENTURE 6

Mystery City

Use the maps of the United States on pages R18 and R20 of your social studies textbook to find the mystery city. Here are the clues:

    This city is not a state capital. It is located along the shore of Puget Sound.

Write the name of the mystery city and the name of the closest major mountain on a sheet of paper.

McGraw-Hill School Division

A Nation Grows

About Alaska

Use the maps of the United States on pages R18 and R20 of your social studies textbook to answer these questions:
- Which bodies of water border Alaska?
- Which countries are closest to Alaska?
- About how many miles from the west coast of Alaska is Mt. McKinley?

Write the answers to these questions as a paragraph about Alaska.

McGraw-Hill School Division

A Nation Grows

GEO ADVENTURE 8

The West Coast

Suppose you know a scientist who wants to study wildlife near the western coast of the United States. The scientist has asked you which states he will have to visit in order to visit all of the coastline. Use the map of the United States on pages R18–R19 of your social studies textbook to help you figure out which states the scientist must visit. Make a list of the states. Next to each state, write the name of a city where the scientist might spend some time.

McGraw-Hill School Division

A Nation Grows

A Mountain State

GEO ADVENTURE 9

Use the map of the United States on pages R20–R21 of your social studies textbook to find this mystery state:

This state is divided by mountains. The Green Mountains separate east and west. Montpelier is the state capital.

Write the name of the mystery state on a sheet of paper. Then make up clues for another mystery state. Be sure to include clues about the landforms in the state.

McGraw-Hill School Division

Latitude and Longitude

Turn to the maps of latitude and longitude on page G5 of your social studies textbook. Then copy these sentences:
- Lines of longitude measure the distance from the prime meridian.
- Lines of latitude are also called meridians.
- Latitude lines extend north and south.

If a sentence states something true, write *T* next to it. If a sentence is false, write *F* next to it. Rewrite each false sentence so it says something true.

McGraw-Hill School Division

A Nation Grows

Continent Chart

GEO ADVENTURE 11

Use the world map on pages R24–R25 of your social studies textbook and the hemisphere maps on page G5 to make a chart of facts about the continents. The chart should include:
- the name of each continent
- the hemispheres in which each continent is located
- the name of two countries on each continent

You can organize the information under the headings *Continent, Location,* and *Country.*

McGraw-Hill School Division

GEO ADVENTURE 12

Mystery Country

Turn to the map of the Western Hemisphere on page R26 of your social studies textbook. Use these clues to find the mystery country:

This country is south of the Equator and west of 60°W longitude. Its capital city is Santiago.

Write the name of the mystery country on a sheet of paper. Then make up clues for another mystery country. Be sure to include latitude and longitude in your clues.

A Nation Grows

McGraw-Hill School Division

More Latitude and Longitude

GEO ADVENTURE 13

Use the maps of latitude and longitude on page 40 of your social studies textbook to answer these questions:
- In which direction do parallels extend?
- What do lines of latitude measure?
- In which directions do lines of longitude extend?
- Where do lines of longitude begin and end?
- At what degree of latitude is the equator?

Write the answers to these questions as a paragraph about latitude and longitude.

McGraw-Hill School Division

A Nation Grows

Visit South America

Use the map of the Western Hemisphere on page R26 of your social studies textbook to follow these directions:

Find the capital of Bolivia. Travel north from this city until you reach the equator. Follow the equator west until you reach another capital city. What city is it?

Write the name of the city and the country. Then list all the countries you passed through along the way.

McGraw-Hill School Division

A Nation Grows

Your State: True or False?

GEO ADVENTURE 15

Turn to the map of the United States on page R18 of your social studies textbook. Copy these sentences:
- My state is west of the Mississippi River.
- My state is less than 200 miles from the 110°W meridian.
- My state is more than 500 miles from the border of Canada.

If a sentence states something true about your state, write *T* next to it. If a sentence is false, write *F* next to it. Then rewrite each false statement to make it true.

McGraw-Hill School Division

A Nation Grows

GEO ADVENTURE 16

Bordering the Pacific Ocean

Turn to the map of the Western Hemisphere on page R26 of your social studies textbook. Name two North American countries that border the Pacific Ocean and are completely east of 90°W longitude. Which South American countries border the Pacific Ocean and are completely south of the equator?

McGraw-Hill School Division

A Nation Grows

Finding Latitude and Longitude

GEO ADVENTURE 17

Suppose you know someone who is learning how to make maps. Your friend needs help with a map of the Western Hemisphere. Use the map of the Western Hemisphere on page R26 of your social studies textbook to help you find these locations:
- 60°N latitude, 150°W longitude
- 30°N latitude, 90°W longitude
- 0° latitude, 60°W longitude

On a sheet of paper, write the name of the city closest to where the lines of latitude and longitude cross.

McGraw-Hill School Division

A Nation Grows

GEO ADVENTURE 18

Five Regions

Turn to the map of Regions of the United States on page 29 of your social studies textbook. Then answer the following questions:
- Of which region are Georgia and Kentucky a part?
- Which states in the West region border the Southwest region?
- Which region extends farthest north?

Write the answers as sentences in a paragraph about regions of the United States.

McGraw-Hill School Division

A Nation Grows

GEO ADVENTURE 19

Sailing the World

Use the world map on pages R24–R25 of your social studies textbook to plan a sailing trip around the world. Begin and end your trip in California. You may not cross any land.

Write a description of the route you would take. Be sure to name the bodies of water you would cross and the directions in which you would travel.

McGraw-Hill School Division

A Nation Grows

Map Scale: True or False?

Turn to the maps of Hawaii on page G7 of your social studies textbook. Then copy these sentences:
- The scales on both maps show only kilometers.
- On both maps the scales show that one inch equals 150 miles.
- On both maps the distance between Kauai and Oahu is about 130 kilometers.

If a sentence states something true, write *T* next to it. If a sentence is false, write *F* next to it. Then rewrite each false statement to make it true.

McGraw-Hill School Division

Across the United States

Turn to the map on pages R18–19 of your social studies textbook. Suppose you know someone who wants to travel across the United States from Canada to Mexico. To make sure she follows a straight route, your friend wants to follow the line of 100°W longitude. Which states will your friend cross? On a sheet of paper, list the states in order.

McGraw-Hill School Division

Georgia and Washington

Use the map of the United States on pages R18–R19 of your social studies textbook to complete a chart.

	Georgia	Washington
borders an ocean		
is north of 40°N latitude		
is east of 90°W longitude		

Copy the chart onto a sheet of paper. Then put a check in the box next to each phrase that describes Georgia or Washington.

McGraw-Hill School Division

A Nation Grows

Native Americans

GEO ADVENTURE 23

Turn to the map of Native Americans in the 1500s on page 62 of your social studies textbook. In which cultural area did the Tlingit live? Which other Native Americans lived in the same area?

In which cultural area did the Creek (Muscogee) live? Which other Native Americans lived nearby?

GEO ADVENTURE 24

Capitals Near 40°N Latitude

Turn to the map of the United States on pages R18–R19 of your social studies textbook. Find 40°N latitude. How many cities are near 40°N latitude? Name the cities that are state capitals.

A Nation Grows

A Pennsylvania Road Map

GEO ADVENTURE 25

Look at the road map of Pennsylvania on page G11 of your social studies textbook. Suppose you know someone who wants to travel from Allentown to Harrisburg. What route should your friend follow?

Suppose your friend wants to go to Johnstown after she visits Harrisburg. Write directions for your friend to follow.

McGraw-Hill School Division

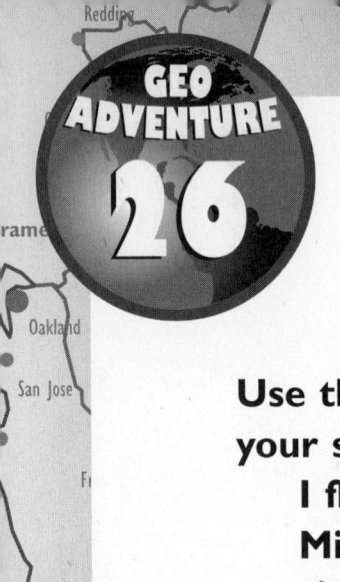

River Riddle

Use the map of the United States on pages R20–R21 of your social studies textbook to solve a river riddle.

I flow from the north to the south. My source is in Minnesota. I empty into the Gulf of Mexico. Which river am I?

A Nation Grows

GEO ADVENTURE 27

Just Plain Facts

Look at the map of the United States on pages R20–R21 of your social studies textbook. Find as many plains as you can. List the names of the plains on a sheet of paper. Write *west* next to those that are west of 90°W longitude. Write *east* next to the plains that are east of 90°W longitude.

McGraw-Hill School Division

A Nation Grows

GEO ADVENTURE 28

East of the Mississippi River

Turn to the physical map of the United States on pages R20–R21 of your social studies textbook. Find the part of the United States that is east of the Mississippi River. Write the words *northern, central,* and *southern* on a sheet of paper. Below each word, write the names of three landforms or physical features found in that part of the eastern United States.

McGraw-Hill School Division

A Nation Grows

Mystery States

GEO ADVENTURE 29

Look at the map of the United States on pages R18–R19 of your social studies textbook. Use this clue to find the mystery states:

These states are crossed by 120°W longitude. Which three states could the mystery state be? Write the names on a sheet of paper. Then write one more clue that would narrow the mystery states from three to one mystery state.

McGraw-Hill School Division

A Nation Grows

GEO ADVENTURE 30

The Amazon River

Turn to the physical map of the Western Hemisphere on page R27 of your social studies textbook. Then answer these questions about the Amazon River:
- In which mountain range is the source of the river?
- In which country is the mouth, or end, of the river?
- Into what body of water does the river empty?

Write the answers as sentences in a paragraph about the Amazon River.

McGraw-Hill School Division

A Nation Grows

Mystery State Clues

Use the map of the United States on pages R18–R19 of your social studies textbook to write clues that would help someone else find a mystery state. Choose a state to write about. Then write a sentence for each clue.

- Tell where the state is located.
- Name other states that are nearby.
- Name the state capital.
- Name any large waterways it has.

McGraw-Hill School Division

Using a Map Scale of Miles

Look at The World Political map on pages R24–R25 of your social studies textbook. Which of the following questions about Africa could you answer only using the map? To answer which questions would you need the scale of miles?

- About how far is it from Morocco to Eqypt?
- Which is farther south—Angola or Libya?
- About how far from South Africa is Tunisia?

McGraw-Hill School Division

Elevation and Relief Maps

GEO ADVENTURE 33

Use the maps on page G10 of your social studies textbook. Then copy these sentences:
- A relief map shows differences in height between areas of land.
- A physical map shows roads and highways.
- An elevation map shows height of land above sea level.

If a sentence states something true, write *T* next to it. If a sentence is false, write *F* next to it. Rewrite each false sentence so it says something true.

A Nation Grows

The Expedition of Magellan

Use the map showing the expedition of Ferdinand Magellan on page 70 of your social studies textbook to finish this paragraph:

Magellan started from Europe and sailed southwest over the _____ Ocean. He sailed along the coast of _____ _____ for a long distance. In 1520 and 1521 he sailed northwest across the _____ Ocean. He reached the _____ Islands in 1521. He _____ but his ship returned to _____.

McGraw-Hill School Division

A Nation Grows

Travel in South America

GEO ADVENTURE 35

Turn to the map of the Western Hemisphere on page R26 of your social studies textbook. Find the capital of Peru. Then answer these questions:
- About how far from the capital of Peru is Bogota, Colombia?
- About how far from Bogota, Colombia is Tucumán, Argentina?
- Which city in Argentina is about 1,000 miles from the capital of Uruguay?

McGraw-Hill School Division

A Nation Grows

GEO ADVENTURE 36

The Ruined City

Suppose you found the journal of an explorer. One of the entries describes the location of a ruined city overgrown with plant life. Look at the map of the world on pages R24–R25 of your social studies textbook. Then read the clues and try to figure out where the city is.

> The city is west of 0° longitude. It is near the equator in a country that borders the Atlantic Ocean.

In which country is the ruined city?

McGraw-Hill School Division

A Nation Grows

Where's My Pen Pal?

GEO ADVENTURE 37

Suppose you received an E-mail from a friend in South America. In the E-mail the friend described her job along the coast of the Pacific Ocean.

Use the map of the Western Hemisphere on page R26 of your social studies textbook to find countries where your friend might live. Make a list of the countries. Next to each country, write the name of the national capital.

McGraw-Hill School Division

South America and the Equator

Find South America on the map of the Western Hemisphere on page R26 of your social studies textbook. Then answer these questions:
- Which countries does the equator cross?
- Which countries in South America are entirely north of the equator?
- Which countries are entirely south of the equator?

Write the answers to these questions as sentences in a paragraph about South America and the equator.

McGraw-Hill School Division

From Central America

GEO ADVENTURE 39

Turn to the map of Central America and the West Indies on page R24 of your social studies textbook. Suppose you know someone who wants to travel from Honduras to Panama. Which countries will your friend cross along the way? List the countries in order on a sheet of paper.

GEO ADVENTURE 40

Mountains of South America

Turn to the map of the Western Hemisphere on page R27 of your social studies textbook. Then answer the following questions:
- Which mountain range is found in South America?
- In which directions does it extend?
- How tall is Mt. Aconcagua?

Write the answers to these questions as sentences in a paragraph about the mountains of South America.

McGraw-Hill School Division

A Nation Grows

A Visit to the Southeast

Use the map of the Southeast on page 33 of your social studies textbook to finish this story:

Mrs. Lopez left _____, the capital of South Carolina, and drove southwest to Atlanta, the capital of _____. Next she drove about _____ miles to Montgomery. Then she drove about 300 miles _____ to Jacksonville, Florida.

Copy the story onto a sheet of paper. Use a number, a direction word, the name of a state, or the name of a city to complete each sentence.

McGraw-Hill School Division

GEO ADVENTURE 42

Mt. Rainier

Turn to the physical map of the United States on page R20 of your social studies textbook. Find Mt. Washington. Then copy these sentences:
- Mt. Washington is the tallest mountain in the United States.
- Mt. Washington is east of Mt. St. Helens.
- Mt. Washington is about 150 miles from the St. Lawrence River.

If a sentence states something true, write *T* next to it. If a sentence is false, write *F* next to it. Rewrite each false sentence so it says something true.

McGraw-Hill School Division

A Nation Grows

An Historical Map: True or False?

Turn to the map of the 13 Colonies on page G11 of your social studies textbook. Then copy these sentences:

- The map shows the United States in the 1700s.
- Maine was part of the New Hampshire colony.
- There were two different groups of colonies in the 1800s.

If a sentence states something true about the map, write *T* next to it. If a sentence is false, write *F* next to it. Rewrite each false sentence to make it true.

McGraw-Hill School Division

A Nation Grows

A 2,000-Mile Trip

Suppose you want to plan a family trip from the national capital of the United States to a city about 2,000 miles away. Use the map of the Western Hemisphere on page R26 of your social studies textbook to plan the trip.

Find a city about 2,000 miles from the national capital. Write the name of the city on a sheet of paper. Then list the cities you would pass through on your way there.

McGraw-Hill School Division

A Nation Grows

Which Map?

Turn to the maps of the Western Hemisphere on pages R26 and R27 of your social studies textbook. On a sheet of paper, write answers to these questions:
- What is the national capital of Nicaragua?
- Which river flows from the Andes Mountains to the Atlantic Ocean?
- Which city is farther north—Anchorage or Iqaluit?

Tell which map helped you answer each question.

McGraw-Hill School Division

GEO ADVENTURE 46

Follow the River

Use the map of the United States on pages R18–R19 of your social studies textbook to help you follow these directions:

Find a city in Idaho that is not the state capital. Follow the river that is north of the city as it flows toward the Pacific Ocean until you come to the Columbia River. Follow the Columbia River west. What is the first city you reach?

McGraw-Hill School Division

A Nation Grows

Fact Sheet for a State

Turn to the map of the United States on pages R18–R19 of your social studies textbook. Choose a state. Then write the following information in sentences on a fact sheet about that state:
- Use latitude and longitude to describe the location of the state.
- List the states or bodies of water that border the state.
- Name the state capital.
- Name other cities in the state.

GEO ADVENTURE 48

The Tropic of Cancer

Look at the map of the world on pages R24–R25 of your social studies textbook. Suppose you know someone who is planning a trip around the world that will begin and end in Mexico. Your friend plans to follow the Tropic of Cancer. Which six countries in Africa will your friend cross? Write the names of the six countries on a sheet of paper.

McGraw-Hill School Division

A Nation Grows

GEO ADVENTURE 49

Mexico: True or False?

Turn to the map of the Western Hemisphere on page R26 of your social studies textbook. Then copy these sentences:
- Most of Mexico is north of 30°N latitude.
- Mexico borders the Atlantic Ocean.
- Most of Mexico is located between 90°W longitude and 120°W longitude.

If a sentence states something true about Mexico, write *T* next to it. If a sentence is false, write *F* next to it. Rewrite each false sentence to make it true.

McGraw-Hill School Division

A Nation Grows

GEO ADVENTURE 50

Reading an Historical Map

Look at the map showing the Conquest of the Inca on page 71 of your social studies textbook. Suppose you lived in Cuzco between 1532 and 1533. How far did you live from Cajamarca? From Quito? From Panama City?

McGraw-Hill School Division

Where Are You Now?

GEO ADVENTURE 51

Use the map of the world on pages R24–R25 of your social studies textbook to help you follow this route: Start in the country that borders the United States to the south. Go east in a straight line to a country in Africa that borders Tunisia and Mali. Then go northwest to a country in Europe at 0° longitude and 40° N latitude. Where are you now?

McGraw-Hill School Division

A Nation Grows

GEO ADVENTURE 52

Mystery Hemisphere

Use the map of the hemispheres on page G5 of your social studies textbook and the world map on pages R24–R25 to find the mystery hemisphere.

This hemisphere includes the countries of South Africa, Peru, and Australia. It does not include Canada or China. Which hemisphere is it?

Write the name of the hemisphere on a sheet of paper. Then make up clues for your own mystery hemisphere. Include the names of countries in your clues.

McGraw-Hill School Division

A Nation Grows

GEO ADVENTURE 53

Off to the Caribbean

Turn to the map of the world on page R24 of your social studies textbook. Suppose you know the captain of a ship. The captain wants to travel from the tip of Florida to Honduras, and then to Puerto Rico. After visiting Puerto Rico, the captain wants to head back to Florida. What route might the captain take to get from place to place? Write directions so that another captain could follow the same route.

McGraw-Hill School Division

A Nation Grows

It's the Mystery State

Use the maps of the United States on pages R18 and R20 of your social studies textbook to find two mystery states.

These states are crossed by the Ouachita Mountains. The Arkansas River passes through both. Write the names of the mystery states on a sheet of paper. Make up a clue that would narrow the mystery states from two to one state.

McGraw-Hill School Division

A Nation Grows

GEO ADVENTURE 55

From Mexico City to Brasília

Find Mexico City on the map of the Western Hemisphere on page R26 of your social studies textbook. Suppose a group of travelers wants to go from Mexico City, Mexico, to Brasília, Brazil.
- In what direction should the group travel?
- How many miles will the group travel?
- Which countries will the group pass through along the way?

McGraw-Hill School Division

A Nation Grows

From Philadelphia to Erie

Use the road map of Pennsylvania on page G11 of your social studies textbook to plan a family trip. Suppose your family wants to travel from Philadelphia to Erie. What are two routes your family can take? Write directions for each route. Be sure to use direction words. Then write a sentence that explains which of the two routes you think your family should take and why.

McGraw-Hill School Division

GEO ADVENTURE 57

Start in Louisiana

Use the map of the United States on pages R18–R19 of your social studies textbook to follow these directions:

Start at the state capital of Louisiana. Travel northeast for about 300 miles until you come to a capital city. Then travel north about 300 miles to a city in Tennessee. Which three cities have you visited?

Now write directions for someone else to follow. Be sure to use direction words and to include the number of miles to travel.

McGraw-Hill School Division

A Nation Grows

Different Maps

Use the maps of the Western Hemisphere on pages R26 and R27 of your social studies textbook to complete a chart.

	political	physical
shows the location of countries		
shows landforms		
has a compass rose		

Copy the chart onto a sheet of paper. Put a check in the box next to each phrase that describes the political map or the physical map.

McGraw-Hill School Division

A Nation Grows

GEO ADVENTURE 59

Find the Cities

Use the map of the Western Hemisphere on page R26 of your social studies textbook to find the following cities:

- Manaus, Brazil
- Galapagos Islands (Ecuador)
- Los Angeles, USA

List the cities on a sheet of paper. Next to each city, write the lines of latitude and longitude that are closest to that city.

McGraw-Hill School Division

New England Colonies

Use the map of the New England Colonies on page 83 of your social studies textbook to answer the following questions:
- What colony was Maine part of?
- Which colonies claimed Vermont?
- Which two colonies were founded the same year?

Write the answers as sentences in a paragraph about the New England colonies.

McGraw-Hill School Division

Your Friend's Trip

GEO ADVENTURE 61

Suppose you have a friend who is traveling from Lima, Peru, to Porto Alegre, Brazil. Use the map of the Western Hemisphere on page R26 of your social studies textbook to describe your friend's trip.

- Which cities and countries does your friend pass through?
- How many miles will your friend have traveled when she reaches Porto Alegre?

McGraw-Hill School Division

A Pen Pal in South America

Suppose someone received a letter from a pen pal in South America. In the letter the pen pal described his home in a city near the eastern border of Argentina.

Use the map of the Western Hemisphere on page R26 of your social studies textbook to find cities where the pen pal might live. Make a list of the cities.

GEO ADVENTURE 63

The Geography of Utah

Find Utah on the map of the United States on page R20 of your social studies textbook. Then copy these sentences:
- The Wasatch Range crosses Utah from east to west.
- The Great Salt Lake Desert is west of the Wasatch Range in Utah.
- Lake Mead is in Southeastern Utah.

If a sentence states something true about Utah, write *T* next to it. If a sentence is false, write *F* next to it. Then rewrite each false statement to make it true.

McGraw-Hill School Division

Farther from St. Louis

Find St. Louis, Missouri, on the map of the United States on pages R18–R19 of your social studies textbook. Then use the map scale to answer this question:

   Which city is farther from St. Louis—Evansville, Illinois, or Cincinnnati, Ohio?

Write the answer on a sheet of paper. Then write a sentence that gives the distance between St. Louis and each of the other cities.

McGraw-Hill School Division

A Nation Grows

The Middle Colonies

GEO ADVENTURE 65

Use the map of the Middle Colonies on page 83 of your social studies textbook to answer the following questions:
- In which colony was Philadelphia located?
- In what year was New York founded?
- What territory is on the map? Which lake is in that territory?

McGraw-Hill School Division

A California Fact Sheet

Find California on the map of the United States on page R20 of your social studies textbook. Then answer these questions:
- What kinds of landforms are found in California?
- Which deserts are found in California?
- Which bodies of water border California or are located within the state?

Write the answers to these questions as sentences on a fact sheet about the geography of California. Be sure to write in complete sentences.

McGraw-Hill School Division

A Nation Grows

Comparing Continents

GEO ADVENTURE 67

Use the physical map of the Western Hemisphere on page R27 of your social studies textbook to complete a chart.

	North America	South America
is mostly west of 60°W		
is crossed by 30°S		
has huge bays and gulfs		

Copy the chart. Then put a check in the box next to each phrase that describes North America or South America.

McGraw-Hill School Division

A Nation Grows

Mystery Country

Use the map of the Western Hemisphere on page R26 of your social studies textbook to find the mystery country.

60°W longitude and 0°S latitude cross in this country.

Write the name of the country on a sheet of paper. Then write a clue for your own mystery country. Be sure to use longitude and latitude in the clue.

McGraw-Hill School Division

120°E Longitude

GEO ADVENTURE 69

Look at the map of the world on pages R24–R25 of your social studies textbook. Find 120°E longitude. Where does this line of longitude meet the equator? Where does 120°E longitude meet 20°S latitude? Where does 120°E longitude meet the Arctic Circle?

GEO ADVENTURE 70

From Atlanta to Denver

Use the maps of the United States on pages R18 and R20 of your social studies textbook to finish this story:

Mei-Li and her family left Atlanta, Georgia, and drove northwest toward Tennessee, crossing the _____ River. At the western border of Tennessee, they crossed the _____ River. Then they drove across the _____ Plains before reaching Denver.

Copy the story onto a sheet of paper. Write the name of a physical feature to complete each sentence.

McGraw-Hill School Division

A Nation Grows

Europe: True or False?

Turn to the map of the world on pages R24–R25 of your social studies textbook. Then copy these sentences:
- Norway is northwest of Poland.
- The United Kingdom is south of France.
- Spain, France, Italy, and Germany border the Mediterranean Sea.

If a sentence states something true about Europe, write *T* next to it. If a sentence is false, write *F* next to it. Rewrite each false sentence so it says something true about Europe.

GEO ADVENTURE 72

Where Is the Netherlands?

Look at the map of the world on pages R24 and R25 of your social studies textbook. Find the Netherlands. Write three sentences describing the country's location. In one of the sentences, tell which countries border the Netherlands.

McGraw-Hill School Division

A Nation Grows

GEO ADVENTURE 73

A Trip from Caracas

Find Caracas, Venezuela, on the map of the Western Hemisphere on page R26 of your social studies textbook. Suppose a group of travelers want to go from Caracas to Montevideo, Uruguay.

- In what direction should the group travel?
- Across which line of longitude will the group travel?
- Which countries will the group pass through along the way?

McGraw-Hill School Division

GEO ADVENTURE 74

A River in South America

Use the map of the Western Hemisphere on page R26 of your social studies textbook to answer these questions:
- What is the largest river system in South America?
- Where is the source of the river?
- Where is its mouth, or end?
- Which countries does the river flow through?

Write the answers to these questions as sentences in a paragraph about the river in South America.

McGraw-Hill School Division

A Nation Grows

Mystery Traveler

Use the map of the United States on pages R18–R19 of your social studies textbook to find the mystery traveler.

The mystery traveler is in a city very near 90°W longitude. In which six cities could she be? Write the names of the cities and states on a sheet of paper. Then write one more clue that would narrow the cities from six to one city.

A Visit to South America

Look at the map of the Western Hemisphere on page R26 of your social studies textbook. Suppose you know someone who wants to travel from the capital of Brazil to the capital of Peru and then to the capital of Paraguay. What route should the person take to get from city to city?

Write directions so that someone else could follow the same route. Be sure to include direction words and the number of miles between cities.

McGraw-Hill School Division

Down the Arkansas River

GEO ADVENTURE 77

Suppose your family took a rafting trip down the Arkansas River. Use the map of the United States on pages R18–R19 of your social studies textbook to describe the trip.

Where is the source of the river? Through which states does the river flow? About how many miles long is it? Write the answers as sentences in a paragraph about your family trip.

A Nation Grows

Mystery State

Turn to the map of the United States on pages R18–R19 of your social studies textbook. Use these clues to find the mystery state:

> This state is bordered on the west by Texas. One of its cities is located near 30°N latitude and 90° longitude.

Write the name of the mystery state and that city on a sheet of paper. Then make up clues for your own mystery state. Include directions and latitude or longitude in your clues.

McGraw-Hill School Division

A Nation Grows

GEO ADVENTURE 79

Comparing Political and Physical Maps

Turn to the maps on pages R26 and R27 of your social studies textbook. Which page shows the western hemisphere? How are the map titles different? What does the map on R27 show that the map on R26 does not show? Which map shows cities? Which map shows countries? Name 3 things that are the same about both maps.

McGraw-Hill School Division

A Nation Grows

GEO ADVENTURE 80

Which Country?

Use the map of the Western Hemisphere on page R26 of your social studies textbook to find the mystery country.

This country is crossed by 120°W longitude and 60°N latitude. Which country is it?

Write clues for your own mystery country. Be sure to use latitude and longitude in one of your clues.

McGraw-Hill School Division

A Nation Grows

110°W Longitude

GEO ADVENTURE 81

Turn to the map of the United States on pages R18–R19 of your social studies textbook. Find 110°W longitude.

Which states are crossed by 110°W longitude? List them on a sheet of paper in order from north to south.

McGraw-Hill School Division

A Nation Grows

GEO ADVENTURE 82

Finding Elevation and Relief

Turn to the elevation and relief maps of Washington on page G10 of your social studies textbook. Find the following cities:

- Spokane
- Seattle
- Everett
- Olympia
- Yakima
- Pullman

List the cities on a sheet of paper. Next to each city, write whether it is located in an area of high, moderate, or low relief.

McGraw-Hill School Division

GEO ADVENTURE 83

A Pen Pal in Africa

Suppose you received a letter from a pen pal in Africa. In the letter the pen pal described her home in a town on the southeast coast of Africa on the Indian Ocean. When you began to write back, you discovered that you had lost your pen pal's address.

Use the map of the world on pages R24–R25 of your social studies textbook to find countries where your pen pal might live. Make a list of the countries.

McGraw-Hill School Division

A Nation Grows

Mystery Hemisphere

Use the map of the hemispheres on page G5 of your social studies textbook and the world map on pages R24–R25 to find the mystery hemisphere.

This hemisphere includes the countries of France, India, and Ethiopia. It does not include the United States or Argentina. Which hemisphere is it?

Write the name of the hemisphere on a sheet of paper. Then make up clues for your own mystery hemisphere. Include the names of countries in your clues.

McGraw-Hill School Division

A Nation Grows

Find the Country

Turn to the world map on pages R24–R25 of your social studies textbook. Use the lines of latitude and longitude to find the locations listed below:
- 20°S latitude, 140°E longitude
- 40°N latitude, 120°E longitude
- 20°N latitude, 80°E longitude
- 20°N latitude, 100°W longitude

On a sheet of paper, write the name of the country at each location.

McGraw-Hill School Division

Mystery Country

Use the map of the world on pages R24–R25 of your social studies textbook to find the mystery country.

This country is on the Mediterranean Sea. It is bordered to the north by Macedonia and to the northwest by Albania. Which country is it?

Write the name of the country on a sheet of paper. Then write clues for your own mystery country. Be sure to use geographic terms in your clues.

McGraw-Hill School Division

GEO ADVENTURE 87

A Great Lakes Vacation

Suppose you know a group of people who are planning a vacation. The people want to visit a state where they will be able to spend time at the shore of one of the Great Lakes. Use the map of the United States on pages R18–R19 of your social studies textbook to help you figure out which states the people might visit. Make a list of the states. Next to each state, write the name of the capital city.

McGraw-Hill School Division

A Nation Grows

Mystery States with a Desert

Turn to the map of the United States on pages R20–R21 of your social studies textbook. Use this clue to find the mystery states:

The Ouachita Mountains cross both of these states. Now look at the map on page R18. Which two states could the mystery states be? Write both names on a sheet of paper. Then write a clue that narrows the mystery states down to one state.

McGraw-Hill School Division

A Nation Grows

A Trip from Bogotá, Colombia

GEO ADVENTURE 89

Use the map of the Western Hemisphere on page R26 of your social studies textbook to finish this story:

Mr. Luna left Bogotá, Colombia, and went _____ to Santiago, Chile. Then he went _____ to Asunción, Paraguay. From Asunción he traveled _____ to La Paz, Bolivia. Finally, he flew _____ to Quito, Ecuador.

Copy the story onto a sheet of paper. Use a direction word to complete each sentence.

GEO ADVENTURE 90

Mystery Countries

Use the map of the Western Hemisphere on page R26 of your social studies textbook to find the mystery countries.

These countries are crossed by the Tropic of Capricorn. Which three countries could they be? Write the names of the countries on a sheet of paper. Then write another clue to narrow the mystery countries from three to one country.

Which Capital City?

Turn to the maps of the United States on pages R18 and R20 of your social studies textbook. Find the state capitals of North Dakota, Maine, and New Mexico.
- Which capital city is close to both mountains and a river?
- What is the name of the mountain range?
- What is the name of the river?

Write the answers to these questions as sentences in a paragraph about the state capital.

GEO ADVENTURE 92

30°N Latitude

Turn to the map of the United States on page R18 of your social studies textbook. Find 110°W longitude.

Which states are crossed by 110°W longitude? List them on a sheet of paper in order from north to south.

McGraw-Hill School Division

# GEO ADVENTURE 93

Reading Inset Maps with Text

Look at the map showing the areas where Spanish explorers went on pages 68 and 69 of your social studies textbook. Which of the following questions can you answer using the inset maps next to the pictures of the explorers?

- What do the lines from the pictures to the big map show?
- Which explorer sailed in the years 1519–1521?
- Which explorer went across a land bridge to the Pacific Ocean in 1513?

McGraw-Hill School Division

A Nation Grows

Indiana's Corn and Dairy Farms

Look at the map of Indiana's Corn and Dairy Farms on page G8 of your social studies textbook. Then answer these questions:
- Where in Indiana is the Dairy-farming area?
- Where in Indiana is the Corn-growing area?
- If you lived near Ft. Wayne, which type of farms would you see?

Use the answers to these questions to write a fact sheet about corn and dairy farms in Indiana.

McGraw-Hill School Division

A Nation Grows

The United States

Turn to the map on pages R22–R23 of your social studies textbook. What is the title of the map?
- Can you find all 50 states?
- What color helps you find them?
- Which 2 states are farthest west?
- Which state is farthest south? Which 2 states are farther south than Texas?
- Which state is closest to Russia?
- About how far away is New Jersey from Hawaii?
- About how far away from California is New Jersey?

McGraw-Hill School Division

GEO ADVENTURE 96

Mystery Traveler

Use the inset map of Central America and the West Indies on page R24 of your social studies textbook to find the mystery traveler.

The mystery traveler is taking a vacation on an island in the Caribbean Sea. This island is east of 80°W longitude and south of 20°N latitude. On which island is he?

A Nation Grows

Powhatan Lands

GEO ADVENTURE 97

Turn to the historical map showing Powhatan Lands About 1600 on page 73 of your social studies textbook. Then answer the following questions:
- What rivers are labeled on the map?
- What large bay is shown?
- Is there a compass rose on the map that shows north, south, east, and west?
- Which river is south of the York River?
- Which people lived north of the Pamunkey?

McGraw-Hill School Division

A Nation Grows

GEO ADVENTURE 98

Closer to Salt Lake City

Find Salt Lake City, Utah, on the map of the United States on page R18 of your social studies textbook. Then use the map scale to answer this question:

Which city is closer to Salt Lake City—Carson City, Nevada, or Boise, Idaho?

Write the answer on a sheet of paper. Then write sentences that tell the distances between Salt Lake City and the other cities.

A Nation Grows

A Canada Fact Sheet

Look at the maps of the Western Hemisphere on pages R26 and R27 of your social studies textbook. Find Canada. Then answer the following questions:
- In what part of Canada are the Coast Mountains located?
- What is the national capital of Canada?
- Which lakes are located north of the Saskatchewan River?

Write the answers as sentences on a fact sheet about Canada.

McGraw-Hill School Division

80°W Longitude

Turn to the map of the world on page R24 of your social studies textbook. Find 80°W longitude.

Which countries are crossed by 80°W longitude? List them on a sheet of paper in order from north to south.

McGraw-Hill School Division

Looking at Borders

GEO ADVENTURE 101

Look at the map of the 50 United States on pages R22–R23 of your social studies textbook.
- Which states have borders on the Pacific Ocean?
- Which states have borders on the Gulf of Mexico?
- Which states have borders on the Great Lakes?
- Which states have borders with other countries?
- Does your state have a border on water?

McGraw-Hill School Division

GEO ADVENTURE 102

A Drive from Lansing, Michigan

Use the map of the United States on pages R18–R19 of your social studies textbook to finish this story:

Tim and his family left their home in Lansing, Michigan, and drove _____ for _____ miles to Norfolk, Virginia. From there they drove _____ for _____ miles to Charlotte, North Carolina. Then they drove _____ for _____ miles to Philadelphia, Pennsylvania.

Copy the story onto a sheet of paper. Use a direction word and the mileage traveled to complete each sentence.

McGraw-Hill School Division

A Nation Grows

Time Zones: True or False?

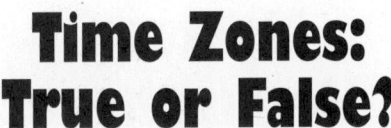

Turn to the time zone map on page 214 of your social studies textbook. Then copy these sentences:
- A time zone is one of the six divisions of Earth used for measuring standard time.
- The time in any zone east of you is later than in your time zone.
- If it is 4:00 P.M. in New York City, it is 3:00 P.M. in Los Angeles.

If a statement is true, write T next to it. Then rewrite each false statement to make it true.

Mystery Hemisphere

Use the map of the hemispheres on page G5 of your social studies textbook and the world map on pages R24–R25 to find the mystery hemisphere.

This hemisphere includes the countries of Canada, Iran, and Japan. It does not include Argentina or Angola. Which hemisphere is it?

Make up clues for your own mystery hemisphere. Include the names of countries in your clues.

McGraw-Hill School Division

A Nation Grows

GEO ADVENTURE 105

Farther from Philadelphia

Find Philadelphia on the road map of Pennsylvania on page G11 of your social studies textbook. Then use the map scale to answer this question:

> Which city is farther from Philadelphia—Bethlehem or Harrisburg?

Write the answer on a sheet of paper. Then write a sentence that tells the distance between Philadelphia and each of the other cities.

The Lewis and Clark Expedition

Turn to the map of the Louisiana Purchase on page 121 of your social studies textbook. Find the route of the Lewis and Clark Expedition. Then answer these questions:
- At which river did the expedition begin?
- Which river did it first follow?
- Where did the expedition start their return trip home?

Write the answers as sentences in a paragraph about the Lewis and Clark Expedition.

McGraw-Hill School Division

A Nation Grows

Visiting the Middle West

Turn to the map of the United States on pages R18–R19 of your social studies textbook. Suppose you have a friend who wants to travel from Columbus, Ohio, to Kansas City, Kansas. In which direction should your friend travel? About how many miles will she have to go?

After visiting Kansas City, your friend wants to travel to a city about 300 miles away. To which city might she go?

A Mediterranean Cruise

Look at the inset map of Europe on page R25 of your social studies textbook. Find Gibraltar near the southern coast of Spain. Suppose you were taking a boat trip from Gibraltar to Sicily and then to Crete. What route would you take to get from place to place? About how many miles would you travel?

McGraw-Hill School Division

A Nation Grows

North from South America

GEO ADVENTURE 109

Turn to the map of the Western Hemisphere on page R26 of your social studies textbook. Find the southern tip of South America. Suppose a friend is traveling north in a straight line from Puenta Arenas, Chile, to the Arctic Ocean. Which countries will your friend pass through? Which bodies of water will she cross?

List the countries and bodies of water in order from south to north.

McGraw-Hill School Division

A Nation Grows

Mystery Traveler

Use the map of the United States on pages R18–R19 of your social studies textbook to find the mystery traveler.

The mystery traveler is in a city just west of 100°W longitude in a state that borders Canada. Where is she?

A Nation Grows

McGraw-Hill School Division

What Time Is It?

Turn to the time zone map on page 214 of your social studies textbook. Find the time zone where you live. Suppose you are planning to make phone calls to friends in Chicago and Los Angeles. What time is it in Chicago right now? What time is it in Los Angeles?

Write your answers as complete sentences. Then explain how you know the time in these different cities.

Cities in South America

Turn to the map of the Western Hemisphere on page R26 of your social studies textbook. Find the capitals of Chile, Argentina, and Guyana.

Write the name of each city on a sheet of paper. Next to each city, write a description of its location using latitude and longitude.

McGraw-Hill School Division

A Nation Grows

A Trail to the West

GEO ADVENTURE 113

Turn to the map of trails to the West on page 124 of your social studies textbook. Imagine that it is the year 1850. You are in Omaha with your Conestoga wagon and a strong team of Clydesdale horses to pull it over the Mormon Trail. Weeks later, you are in Fort Laramie. Write a letter to tell a friend what you saw on the trail.

GEO ADVENTURE 114

Reading an Inset Map for Details

Find the map of the world on pages R24 and R25 of your social studies textbook. Then look at the inset map of Central America and West Indies on R24. How can you tell where this map area is on the world map?

- Which map could you use to find Colombia?
- Which map could you use to find Jamaica and Puerto Rico or Panama?
- Why do you think the mapmakers (cartographers) did not put the names of the Central American countries on the world map?

McGraw-Hill School Division

A Nation Grows

Elevation and Relief

Turn to the elevation and relief maps on page G10 of your social studies textbook. Then copy these sentences:
- How do you know that both maps are of the same place?
- What is the same about both maps?
- What is different?
- Which map looks bumpy?
- Which map looks smooth but shows how high the land is?

McGraw-Hill School Division

Railroads in the West

Look at the map of Railroads in the West on page 205 of your social studies textbook. Suppose you are the engineer on a train going west in 1890. Your run started in Chicago. What two cities are on the map of your route before you get to San Francisco? Are you going to go over any mountain ranges? Check the map on pages R20 and R21 and write their names.

Texas and California

Use the map of the United States on pages R18–R19 of your social studies textbook and the time zone map on page 214 to complete the chart.

	Texas	California
is in the Central Time Zone		
is crossed by 100°W longitude		
is in the Pacific Time Zone		

Copy the chart onto a sheet of paper. Put a check in the box next to each phrase that describes Texas or California.

McGraw-Hill School Division

Latitude and Longitude

Turn to the world map on pages R24–R25 of your social studies textbook. Use the lines of latitude and longitude to find the following locations:
- Tropic of Cancer, 100°W longitude
- Tropic of Cancer, 40°E longitude
- 20°S latitude, 20°E longitude
- 0° latitude, 20°E longitude

On a sheet of paper, write the name of the country at each location.

GEO ADVENTURE 119

A Trip from Nome

Look at the map of the United States on pages R18–R19 of your social studies textbook and the time zone map on page 214. Suppose you travel from Nome, Alaska, to Seattle, Washington. Then you go on to Orlando, Florida.

Which time zones will you pass through along the way?

McGraw-Hill School Division

A Nation Grows

GEO ADVENTURE 120

Mystery Traveler in Pennsylvania

Use the road map of Pennsylvania on page G11 of your social studies textbook to find out which cities the mystery traveler visited.

The mystery traveler started at a city on Lake Erie. She drove south on Interstate 79 until it crossed Interstate 80. Then she drove east on Interstate 80 until she reached state highway 219. She traveled south on that highway about 60 miles.

On a sheet of paper, write the names of the cities where the mystery traveler started and ended her trip.

McGraw-Hill School Division

A Nation Grows

GEO ADVENTURE 121

Which Distance Is Longer?

Use the map of the Western Hemisphere on page R26 of your social studies textbook to answer this question:
   Which distance is longer?
   From Fairbanks, Alaska, to Monterrey, Mexico, or from Monterrey, Mexico, to the Falkland Islands (off the southern tip of South America)?
Write the answer on a sheet of paper. Then write a sentence that tells the number of miles between the two cities in each pair.

McGraw-Hill School Division

A Nation Grows

Mystery Traveler Code

Turn to the map of the United States on pages R22 and R23 of your social studies textbook. Suppose you went to these places:

40°N latitude, 110°W longitude; then to 30°N latitude, 100°W longitude; then to 40°N latitude, 80°W longitude; and finally to 20°N latitude, 155°W longitude. Which states did you visit?

McGraw-Hill School Division

A Nation Grows

Using a Map Key

Turn to the map of Indiana's Corn and Dairy Farms on page G8 of your social studies textbook. Which of the following questions can you answer using the map key?
- Which products are produced in Muncie?
- What is the capital of Indiana?
- About how far from the state capital is Bedford?
- Which river forms the southern border of Indiana?

McGraw-Hill School Division

A National Forest

Look at the map of the Francis Marion National Forest on page G8 of your social studies textbook. Answer these questions:
- In which state is the forest located?
- How many campgrounds are there?
- In which direction is Cordesville?

Write the answers as sentences on a fact sheet about Francis Marion National Forest. Then add one more fact that you can learn from the map.

McGraw-Hill School Division

A Nation Grows

Time Chart

Use the map of the United States on pages R18–R19 of your social studies textbook and the time zone map on page 214 to complete this chart.

City	Time Zone	Time
Reno, Nevada		1:00 P.M.
Madison, Wisconsin		
Memphis, Tennessee		

Copy the chart onto a sheet of paper. Then find each city. Suppose it is 1:00 P.M. in Reno. Figure out the time in each of the other cities and fill it in on the chart.

GEO ADVENTURE 125

A Nation Grows

A Cattle Trail

Turn to the map of Cattle Trails in the West on page 211 of your social studies textbook. Suppose a rancher left San Antonio, Texas, in 1876 and followed the Western Trail north. In which state did the rancher end up? In which city along the way could the rancher have begun a railroad trip?

McGraw-Hill School Division

A Nation Grows

GEO ADVENTURE 127

From Canada to Guatemala

Suppose you have a friend who is traveling on a bus from Ottawa, Canada, to Guatemala City, Guatemala. Use the map of the Western Hemisphere on page R26 of your social studies textbook to describe your friend's trip.

- Which countries will your friend pass through?
- About how many miles will your friend travel before a stop in Monterrey, Mexico?
- About how many miles will your friend still have to travel after the stop in Mexico?

McGraw-Hill School Division

GEO ADVENTURE 128

Trails: True or False?

Turn to the map of trails to the West on page 124 of your social studies textbook. Then copy these sentences:
- Donner Pass was located along the Oregon Trail.
- Salt Lake City was west of Split Rock.
- The California Trail led to San Francisco.
- Santa Fe was north of Soda Springs.

If a sentence states something true, write *T* next to it. If a sentence is false, write *F* next to it. Rewrite each false sentence to make it true.

McGraw-Hill School Division

A Nation Grows

GEO ADVENTURE 129

Facts from Different Maps

Turn to the political map of the United States on pages R18–R19 of your social studies textbook. Find Georgia. What can you learn about Georgia by studying the map? On a sheet of paper, write as many facts as you can.

Then turn to the physical map of the United States on pages R20–R21. What more can you learn about Georgia from this map? Add more facts to your list.

McGraw-Hill School Division

A Nation Grows

Find the Cities

Use the map of the Western Hemisphere on page R26 of your social studies textbook to find these cities:
- Quito, Ecuador
- New Orleans, United States
- Porto Alegre, Brazil

List the cities on a sheet of paper. Next to each city, write the lines of latitude that are closest to that city. What might you guess about the climate of Quito? Do you think New Orleans and Porto Alegre might have similar climates? Why?

McGraw-Hill School Division

A Nation Grows

Where Are These Cities?

GEO ADVENTURE 131

Use the map of the United States on pages R18–R19 of your social studies textbook to find these cities:
- Sacramento, California
- Providence, Rhode Island
- Honolulu, Hawaii

List the cities on a sheet of paper. Next to each city, write the numbers of the lines of latitude and longitude that are closest to that city.

McGraw-Hill School Division

A Nation Grows

GEO ADVENTURE 132

Charleston, West Virginia

Find Charleston, West Virginia, on the map of the United States on pages R18–R19 of your social studies textbook. Then answer these questions:
- Which city is closest to Charleston?
- Which city is west of Charleston?
- Which city is south of Charleston?

Choose from the following cities for the answers:
Kansas City, Kansas
Richmond, Virginia
Miami, Florida

McGraw-Hill School Division

A Nation Grows

Follow the Directions

Use the map of the United States on pages R18–R19 of your social studies textbook to follow these directions:

Start at 40°N latitude, 110°W longitude. Go 30 degrees east. Then go 10 degrees south. Now go 10 degrees west. Then go 10 degrees north.

Which city are you close to? What is the closest latitude and longitude of the city?

GEO ADVENTURE 133

McGraw-Hill School Division

A Nation Grows

Mystery Traveler

Use the maps of the Western Hemisphere on pages R26 and R27 of your social studies textbook to find out where the mystery traveler went.

The mystery traveler started his trip in Buenos Aires, Argentina. He followed the Paraná River to a city in Paraguay. Then he traveled west nearly 800 miles across the Andes to a city on the Pacific Ocean.

On a sheet of paper, write the names of the two cities the mystery traveler visited.

McGraw-Hill School Division

A Nation Grows

Mystery Hemisphere

Use the map of the hemispheres on page G5 of your social studies textbook and the world map on pages R24–R25 to find the mystery hemisphere.

This hemisphere includes the countries of Canada, Uruguay, and Haiti. It does not include Indonesia, Iraq, or Sudan. Which hemisphere is it?

Write the name of the hemisphere on a sheet of paper. Then make up clues for your own mystery hemisphere. Include the names of countries in your clues.

GEO ADVENTURE 136

Farthest Apart

Use the map of the Western Hemisphere on page R26 of your social studies textbook to answer this question:
   Which cities are farthest apart?
   Mexico City, Mexico, and Caracas, Venezuela?
   Washington, D.C., and Winnipeg, Canada?
   Havana, Cuba, and Bogota, Colombia?
Write the answer on a sheet of paper.

McGraw-Hill School Division

A Nation Grows

A Northern Border

GEO ADVENTURE 137

Turn to the map of the United States on pages R18–R19 of your social studies textbook. Use the map scale to answer these questions:
- How long is the northern border of North Carolina?
- Is it longer or shorter than the northern border of Alabama?
- How much longer or shorter is it?

McGraw-Hill School Division

A Nation Grows

GEO ADVENTURE 138

Start in Ohio

Use the map of the United States on pages R18–R19 of your social studies textbook to follow these directions:
Start at the state capital of Ohio. Travel southeast for about 450 miles to a city on the coast of Virginia. Then travel about 600 miles to the capital of a state that borders Arkansas to the west. Which three cities have you visited?

McGraw-Hill School Division

A Nation Grows

Mystery Country

Use the world map on pages R24–R25 of your social studies textbook to find the mystery country.

    This country is an island in the Indian Ocean.
    It is crossed by 20°S latitude and the Tropic of Capricorn.

Write the name of the mystery country on a sheet of paper. Then make up clues for your own mystery country. Include geographic terms and latitude or longitude in your clues.

McGraw-Hill School Division

A Nation Grows

GEO ADVENTURE 140

Plan a River Trip

Suppose a group of people were planning to take a river trip from Duluth, Minnesota, to New Orleans, Louisiana. Use the maps of the United States on pages R18 and R20 of your social studies textbook to help plan the trip.

- Which river would the group follow?
- Which cities would the group pass along the way?
- What kinds of landforms might the group see?

McGraw-Hill School Division

A Nation Grows

What Am I?

Use the physical map of the United States on page R20 of your social studies textbook to solve this riddle:

> I am a body of water south and west of the Wasatch Range at the headwaters of the Colorado River. I am east of Death Valley. What am I?

Write the answer on a sheet of paper. Then use the map to make up a riddle of your own.

McGraw-Hill School Division

GEO ADVENTURE 142

Mystery Traveler Code

Turn to the inset map of Europe on page R25 of your social studies textbook. Suppose the mystery traveler gave you this coded message about a trip to Europe:

I'm going to 60°N latitude, 10°E longitude; then to 50°N latitude, 20°E longitude; and finally to 40°N latitude, 30°E longitude.

What countries in Europe does the mystery traveler plan to visit? Write them in order on a sheet of paper.

McGraw-Hill School Division

A Nation Grows

GEO ADVENTURE 143

The Great Basin

Turn to the physical map of the United States on page R20 of your social studies textbook. Then answer these questions about the Mojave Desert:

- Which mountains are north and west of the Mojave Desert?
- Which desert is south and east of the Mojave Desert?
- What areas are north of the Mojave Desert?

Write the answers as sentences in a paragraph about the Mojave Desert.

McGraw-Hill School Division

Which Is Nearer?

Look at the map of the United States on pages R18–R19 of your social studies textbook. Find Fort Wayne, Indiana. Then use the map scale to answer this question:

Which is nearer to Fort Wayne—Lincoln, Nebraska, or Harrisburg, Pennsylvania?

Write the answer on a sheet of paper. Then write a sentence that tells the distance between Fort Wayne and each of the other places.

McGraw-Hill School Division

A Nation Grows

Following the Tropic of Cancer

GEO ADVENTURE 145

Turn to the map of the world on pages R24–R25 of your social studies textbook. Suppose you know someone who plans to follow the Tropic of Cancer around the world. Your friend plans to begin and end his trip in Algeria. He will travel west. Which countries and bodies of water will your friend cross?

McGraw-Hill School Division

A Nation Grows

GEO ADVENTURE 146

A Pen Pal in Europe

Suppose your friend received a letter from a pen pal in Europe. In the letter her pen pal described her life in a town near the coast of the Mediterranean Sea.

Use the inset map of Europe on page R25 of your social studies textbook to find countries where your friend's pen pal might live. Make a list of the countries.

McGraw-Hill School Division

A Nation Grows

Mystery City

Use the map of the United States on pages R18–R19 of your social studies textbook and the time zone map on page 214 to find the mystery city. Here are the clues:

When it is 10 A.M. in this state capital, it is 11 A.M. in Washington, D.C. This city is located on the Arkansas River. What is the mystery city?

Write the name of the mystery city. Then write clues for your own mystery city. Use the time zone map to help you write one of your clues.

McGraw-Hill School Division

A Nation Grows

Facts About Peru

Turn to the political map of the Western Hemisphere on page R26 of your social studies textbook. Find Peru. What can you learn about Peru by studying the map? Write as many facts as you can.

Then look at the physical map of the Western Hemisphere on page R27. What more can you learn about Peru from this map? Add more facts to your list.

McGraw-Hill School Division

Nigeria Fact Sheet

GEO ADVENTURE 149

Turn to the world map on pages R24–R25 of your social studies textbook. Suppose you are making a fact sheet for a group of travelers on their way to Nigeria. Write the following information on the fact sheet:
- Use latitude and longitude to describe the location of Nigeria.
- Describe a route the travelers might take to get to Nigeria from the United States.
- Name some of the countries that border Nigeria.

McGraw-Hill School Division

A Nation Grows

GEO ADVENTURE 150

The World Traveler

Use the map of the world on pages R24–R25 of your social studies textbook to follow the path of the world traveler.

> The world traveler started his trip in a country that borders Laos, China, and the Pacific Ocean. Then he traveled north in a straight line until he reached the Arctic Circle. Finally, he followed the Arctic Circle east to 160°W longitude.

In which country is the world traveler now? Which other countries did he visit?

McGraw-Hill School Division

A Nation Grows

Answer Key

1. The maps should accurately reflect the shape of the state in which students live, include a compass rose, and include a label that shows the correct location of the state capital. The maps should be colored and have an appropriate title.

2. Colorado; to check the accuracy of their clues, you may want to have students read their clues aloud and solve one another's mystery states. At least one clue should contain a direction word and distances in miles.

3. Students should accurately list the states they would cross in order if they were traveling from their state capital to Richmond, Virginia. Students should also provide the capital of each state on the list.

4. Denver, Colorado: 40°N latitude, 110°W longitude; Austin, Texas: 30°N latitude, 100°W longitude; Pittsburgh, Pennsylvania: 40°N latitude, 80°W longitude

5. South Africa

6. Seattle: Mt. Rainier

7. the Arctic Ocean, the Bering Sea, and the Bering Strait; Russia, Canada; about 500 miles. The paragraph should mention that Alaska is a state and in three or four sentences include the answers just given.

8. The list should include Washington, Oregon, and California. Some students may include Alaska. Cities where the scientist may spend some time include: Olympia, Seattle, Eugene, Salem, Long Beach, San Diego, and Nome.

9. Vermont; to check the accuracy of their clues, you may want to have students read their clues aloud and solve one another's mystery state. At least one clue should contain information about landforms.

10. The first sentence is true. The other two sentences can be rewritten as follows: lines of longitude are called meridians; latitude lines extend east and west.

11. Continent: Africa, Antarctica, Asia, Australia, Europe, North America, South America
Location: Northern—Asia, Europe, Africa, North America, and part of South America
Southern—South America, Antarctica, Africa, Australia, and part of Asia
Western—North America, South America, and part of Antarctica
Eastern—Africa, Europe, Asia, Australia, and part of Antarctica
Country: Africa—Egypt and Ethiopia, among others
Asia—Russia and China, among others
Australia—Australia and New

Zealand, among others
Europe—France and Spain, among others
North America—United States and Mexico, among others
South America—Brazil and Argentina, among others
Antarctica

12. Chile; to check the accuracy of their clues, you may want to have students read their clues aloud and solve one another's mystery countries. At least one clue should contain information about latitude and longitude.

13. east and west; measure the distance north and south of the equator; North and South; North Pole and South Pole; 0°

14. Quito, Equador; Brazil and Colombia are passed through along the way.

15. Students' answers should accurately reflect the location of their state.

16. North American countries that border the Pacific Ocean and are completely east of 90°W longitude include El Salvador, Honduras, Nicaragua, Costa Rica, and Panama. South American countries that border the Pacific Ocean and are completely south of the equator include Peru and Chile.

17. 60°N latitude, 150° W longitude—Anchorage, Alaska; 30°N latitude, 90°W longitude—New Orleans, Louisiana; 0° latitude, 60°W longitude—Manaus, Brazil

18. Southeast; California, Nevada, Utah, Colorado; Northeast

19. Students' route descriptions may include the following bodies of water: Pacific Ocean, Atlantic Ocean, Indian Ocean, Arctic Ocean.

20. The third sentence is true. The other two sentences can be written as follows: The scales on both maps show miles and kilometers. The scale on one map shows one inch as 260 miles and the scale on the other shows one inch as 130 miles.

21. North Dakota, South Dakota, Nebraska, Kansas, Oklahoma, and Texas

22. Borders an ocean—Washington; is north of 40°N latitude—Washington; is east of 90°W longitude—Georgia

23. The Northwest Coast; Students' answers may include the Chinook, the Aleut, and the Ahtena. The Eastern Woodlands; Students' answers may include the Natchez, the Chickasaw, and the Tuscarora among others.

24. Answers may include: 10 cities; Denver, Colorado; Springfield, Illinois; Indianapolis, Indiana; Columbus, Ohio; Harrisburg, Pennsylvania; Trenton, New Jersey.

25. Interstate 78. Directions to Johnstown should include: travel west from Harrisburg on Interstate 81; then follow Interstate 76 west to Interstate 70; follow Interstate 70 west; then travel north on route 219 to Johnstown.

A Nation Grows·Answer Key

26. Mississippi River

27. The Atlantic Coastal Plain—East, Gulf Coastal Plain—East and West, Central Plains—East and West, Interior Plains—West, Great Plains—West

28. Students might write the following: under *northern*—White Mountains, Mt. Washington, Green Mountains, Cape Cod, Hudson River, Long Island, Lake Ontario, Lake Erie, Lake Huron, Lake Michigan, Lake Superior; under *central*—Allegheny Plateau, Appalachian Mountains, Ohio River, Wabash River, Mt. Mitchell, Delaware Bay, Chesapeake Bay, Potomac River; under *southern*—Savannah River, Appalachian Mountains, Chatahoochee River, Alabama River, Mobile Bay, Gulf Coastal Plain, Florida Keys, Straits of Florida, Lake Okeechobee.

29. California, Oregon, Washington; to check the accuracy of their clues, you may want to have students read their clues aloud and find one another's mystery states.

30. Students' paragraphs should include the following information: the source of the Amazon River is in the Andes Mountains; the mouth of the Amazon River is in Brazil; the Amazon River empties into the Atlantic Ocean.

31. Students' answers should include location using latitude and longitude, bordering states, the state's capital, and any major passages of water. To check the accuracy of their clues, you may want to have students read their clues aloud and find one another's mystery states.

32. About 1,500 miles. Angola; over 4,000 miles.

33. The first and third sentences are true. The second sentence can be rewritten as follows: A physical map is a map that highlights the Earth's natural features.

34. Atlantic; South America; Pacific; Philippine; died, Europe.

35. Bogota, Colombia is about 1,000 miles from Lima, Peru. Bogota, Colombia is about 2,000 miles from Tucumán, Argentina. Comodoro Rivadavia is about 1,000 miles from Montevideo. You might suggest students use a ruler or map scale strip when determining distances.

36. Brazil

37. Colombia—Bogotá;
    Equador—Quito;
    Peru—Lima;
    Chile—Santiago.

38. Students' paragraphs should include the following information: the equator crosses Ecuador, Colombia, and Brazil; Venezuela, Guyana, Suriname, and French Guiana are entirely north of the equator; Peru, Bolivia, Chile, Argentina, Paraguay, and Uruguay are entirely south of the equator.

39. The friend will go through Honduras, Nicaragua, Costa Rica, and Panama.

40. Students' paragraphs should include the following information: the Andes range is found in

South America; the Andes extend from north to south; Mt. Aconcagua is 22,834 feet tall.

41. Columbia; Georgia; 150; south

42. The second and third sentences are true. The first sentence can be rewritten as follows: Mt. Washington is not the tallest mountain in the United States. Mt. McKinley is the tallest mountain in the United States.

43. The second and third sentences are false and can be rewritten as follows: Maine was part of the Massachusetts colony; there were three different groups of colonies in the 1700s.

44. Students' directions should accurately describe how to get from Washington, D.C., to a city that is about 2,000 miles away. Students should list the cities and/or countries they would pass through along the way. You might suggest students use a ruler or map scale strip when determining distances.

45. Managua; Amazon River; Iqaluit; political, physical, political

46. Portland, Oregon

47. Students' answers should include the latitude and longitude of the state, the states or bodies of water that border the state, the state's capital, and other cities in the state.

48. Morocco, Mauritania, Mali, Algeria, Libya, Egypt

49. The third sentence is true. The other sentences can be rewritten as follows: most of Mexico is south of 30°N latitude; Mexico borders the Pacific Ocean, the Gulf of Mexico, Guatemala, Belize, and the United States.

50. About 600 miles; 1,000 miles; about 1,750 miles.

51. Begin in Mexico; go east to Algeria; go northwest to Spain.

52. Southern Hemisphere; to check the accuracy of their clues, you may want to have students read their clues aloud and find one another's mystery hemispheres.

53. Students should accurately describe the following route: travel southeast from the tip of Florida to Cuba; from Cuba, southeast to Barbados; from Barbados, northwest to Florida.

54. Arkansas to Oklahoma; to check the accuracy of their clues, you may want to have students read their clues aloud and find one another's mystery states.

55. Southeast; about 3,500 miles; the group will pass through Guatemala, Honduras, Nicaragua, Costa Rica, Panama, Colombia, and Brazil.

56. Route 1: from Philadelphia take Interstate 76 west; then take Interstate 79 north to Erie. Route 2: take state highway 422 north to state highway 322; take state highway 322 west to Interstate 80; take Interstate 80 west to Interstate 79; take Interstate 79 north to Erie.

57. Baton Rouge, Louisiana; Montgomery, Alabama; Nashville, Tennessee. To check the accuracy of their directions,

you may want to have students listen to and follow one another's directions.

58. Shows the location of countries–political; shows landforms–physical; has a compass rose–political, physical

59. Manaus, Brazil: 0° latitude, 60°W longitude; Galapagos Islands (Ecuador): 0° latitude, 90°W longitude; Los Angeles, USA: 30°N latitude, 120°W longitude

60. Massachusetts; New Hampshire and New York; Connecticut and Rhode Island.

61. Students might indicate that their friend is passing through Lima, Peru; La Paz and Sucre, Bolivia; and Asuncion, Paraguay. The friend will have traveled almost 2,000 miles. You might suggest students use a ruler or map scale strip when determining distances.

62. Comodora Rivadavia; Mar del Plata; La Plata; Buenos Aires

63. The second sentence is true. The other sentences can be rewritten as follows. The Wasatch Range crosses Utah from north to south. Lake Mead is in southeast Nevada.

64. Cincinnati, Ohio. Cincinnati is about 300 miles from St. Louis, Missouri, and Evansville, Illinois, is about 150 miles from St. Louis, Missouri.

65. Pennsylvania; 1664; The French Territory; Lake Ontario

66. Students' fact sheets should include the following information: mountains, deserts, and valleys are some of the landforms found in California; the Mojave Desert and the Sonora Desert are found in California; the Pacific Ocean borders the state and the San Joaquin River, the Sacramento River, and the Salton Sea are located within California.

67. is mostly west of 60°W–North America; is crossed by 30°S–South America; has huge bays and gulfs–North America

68. Brazil; to check the accuracy of their clues, you may want to have students read their clues aloud and find one another's mystery countries.

69. Indonesia; Australia; Russia

70. Tennessee River; Mississippi River; Great Plains

71. The first sentence is true. The other sentences can be rewritten as follows: the United Kingdom is north of France; Spain, France, Italy, and Greece border the Mediteranean Sea.

72. Students might write sentences like these: The countries that border the Netherlands are Belgium and Germany. The Netherlands also borders the North Sea. The Netherlands is located east of 0° longitude and north of 50°N latitude.

73. Southeast across 60°W longitude; Venezuela, Brazil, Paraguay, Argentina, Uruguay

74. Students' paragraphs should include the following information: the Amazon is South America's largest river system; the source of the river is in the

Andes Mountains; the mouth of the river is located in Brazil; the Amazon River flows through Colombia, Peru, Bolivia, and Brazil.

75. Cities and states could include: New Orleans, Louisiana; Memphis, Tennessee; St. Louis, Missouri; Springfield, Illinois; Peoria, Illinois; Davenport, Iowa; Madison, Wisconsin; to check the accuracy of their clues, you may want to have students read their clues aloud and solve one another's mystery states. At least one clue should contain a direction word and distances in miles.

76. Students should accurately describe the following route: from Brasília, Brazil, travel west about 2,000 miles to Lima, Peru; from Lima, travel southeast about 1,500 miles to Asunción, Paraguay. You might suggest students use a ruler or map scale strip when determining distances.

77. Students' paragraphs should include the following information: the source of the Arkansas River is in Colorado; from Colorado the river flows southeast through Kansas, Oklahoma, and Arkansas, where it meets the Mississippi River; the Arkansas River is about 1,000 miles long.

78. New Orleans; Louisiana; to check the accuracy of their clues, you may want to have students read their clues aloud and find one another's mystery states.

79. R6 and R7 both picture Western Hemisphere; R6 shows political divisions; R7 shows physical features, such as mountains, plains, and valleys; R6 shows cities and countries. Both maps are drawn to the same scale, both show the same land masses and the relationship of land to water.

80. Canada; to check the accuracy of their clues, you may want to have students read their clues aloud and find one another's mystery countries.

81. Arizona, Utah, Wyoming, Montana

82. Spokane—moderate relief; Seattle—low relief; Olympia—low relief; Yakima—low relief; Everett—low relief; Pullman—moderate relief

83. Somalia, Kenya, Tanzania, Mozambique, South Africa

84. Eastern Hemisphere; to check the accuracy of their clues, you may want to have students read their clues aloud and find one another's mystery hemispheres.

85. 20°S latitude, 140°E longitude: Australia; 40°N latitude, 120°E longitude: China; 20°N latitude, 80°E longitude: India; 20°N latitude, 100°W longitude: Mexico

86. Greece; to check the accuracy of their clues, you may want to have students read their clues aloud and find one another's mystery countries.

87. Michigan—Lansing; Wisconsin—Madison; Illinois—Springfield; Indiana—Indianapolis; Ohio—Columbus; Pennsylvania—Harrisburg; New York—Albany

88. Oklahoma and Arkansas; to check the accuracy of their

clues, you may want to have students read their clues aloud and find one another's mystery states.

89. south; northeast; northwest; northwest

90. Chile, Paraguay, Brazil; to check the accuracy of their clues, you may want to have students read their clues aloud and find one another's mystery countries.

91. Students' paragraphs should include the following information: Santa Fe is close to both mountains and a river; Santa Fe is close to the Rocky Mountains; Santa Fe is close to the Rio Grande River.

92. Montana, Wyoming, Utah, Arizona

93. Where the map areas in the inset maps are found on the main map; Cortés; Balboa

94. Students' fact sheets should include the following information: dairy farms can be found in northeastern, northwestern, and parts of southern Indiana; farms that grow corn are found in the central part of the state; near Ft. Wayne, a person would see dairy farms.

95. the 50 United States; yes, all 50 are on the map; they are green; Hawaii and Alaska are farthest west; Florida; Hawaii and Florida; Alaska; 6,000 miles; 3,000 miles.

96. Jamaica

97. Potomac, Rappahannock, York, and James Rivers; Chesapeake Bay; there is a compass rose; James River; Arrohateck; Mattaponi.

98. Boise, Idaho. Boise is about 300 miles from Salt Lake City, Utah. Carson City, Nevada, is about 450 miles away. You might suggest students use a ruler or map scale strip when determining distances.

99. Students' fact sheets should include the following information: the Coast Mountains are located in western Canada; the national capital of Canada is Ottawa; Great Slave Lake and Great Bear Lake are located north of the Saskatchewan River.

100. Canada, the United States, Cuba, Panama, Ecuador, Peru

101. Alaska, Hawaii, Washington, Oregon, California; Florida, Alabama, Mississippi, Louisiana, Texas; New York, Pennsylvania, Ohio, Michigan, Indiana, Illinois, Wisconsin, Minnesota; Maine, New Hampshire, Vermont, New York, Minnesota, North Dakota, Montana, Idaho, Washington, Alaska to the north, California, Arizona, New Mexico, Texas to the south; Answers will vary, rivers may be used in the answer.

102. southeast; 600; southwest; 300; northeast; 450

103. The second sentence is true. The other sentences can be rewritten as follows: a time zone is one of the 24 divisions of Earth used for measuring standard time; if it is 4:00 P.M. in New York City, it is 1:00 P.M. in Los Angeles.

104. Northern Hemisphere; to check the accuracy of their clues, you may want to have students read their clues aloud and find one another's mystery hemispheres.

105. Harrisburg. Harrisburg is about 90 miles from Philadelphia. Bethlehem is about 50 miles from Philadelphia. You might suggest students use a ruler or map scale strip when determining distances.

106. Students' paragraphs should include the following information: the Lewis and Clark Expedition began at the Mississippi River; the expedition first followed the Missouri River; the expedition began their trip home at the Pacific Coast.

107. Southwest; about 600 miles. After Kansas City, the friend might visit Oklahoma City, Oklahoma.

108. Students should accurately describe the following route: from Gibraltar travel east to the southeastern tip of Sicily; from Sicily travel southeast to Crete; 1,500 miles.

109. Argentina, Chile, Peru, Brazil, Colombia, Venezuela, Caribbean Sea, Dominican Republic, Atlantic Ocean, United States, Canada, Baffin Bay, Greenland, Canada

110. Bismarck, North Dakota

111. Students' responses and explanations should reflect their understanding that they add an hour for each time zone east of where they are and subtract an hour for each time zone west of where they are.

112. Santiago, Chile: south of 30°S latitude and west of 60°W longitude; Buenos Aires, Argentina: south of 30°S latitude and east of 60°W longitude; Georgetown, Guyana: north of 0° latitude (equator) and east of 60°W longitude

113. Students' letters should include the difficulty and hardship many settlers experienced on the trails. They would have seen many Native Americans who developed the trails in the 1880s for the fur trappers called Mountain Men. They would have seen that many wagons had to leave behind much of their furniture in Chimney Rock to lighten their load so they could continue on. Once at Fort Laramie they would have seen many people continue on to the California Trail in search of gold.

114. The outline of the inset map appears on the main map; main and inset maps; inset map; the scale of the main map is too large for names to be legible.

115. Because both maps have the name of the state in the upper left-hand corner and both maps have the same boundries highlighted; Both are physical maps; One is a relief map and the other an elevation map; The relief map because it shows the difference in height between areas of land; The elevation map.

116. Omaha and Promontory Point; Yes, the Rocky Mountains, the Wasatch Range, and the Sierra Nevada.

117. is in the Central Time Zone—Texas; is crossed by 100°W latitude—Texas; is in the Pacific Time Zone—California

118. Tropic of Cancer, 100°W longitude: Mexico; Tropic of Cancer, 40°E longitude: Saudi Arabia; 20°S latitude, 20°E longitude:

Namibia; 0° latitude, 20°E longitude: Congo

119. You would travel through the Alaska Time Zone, the Pacific Time Zone, the Mountain Time Zone, the Central Time Zone, and the Eastern Time Zone.

120. Erie; Johnstown

121. The distance from Monterrey to the Falkland Islands is longer. It is about 5,500 miles. The distance from Fairbanks to Monterrey is about 4,000 miles. You might suggest students use a ruler or map scale strip when determining distances.

122. Utah, Texas, Pennsylvania, and Hawaii

123. The first and second sentences can be answered using the map key.

124. Students' fact sheets should include the following information: the Francis Marion National Forest is located in South Carolina; the park has three campgrounds; west.

125. Reno, Nevada—Pacific Time Zone; Madison, Wisconsin—Central Time Zone, 3 P.M.; Memphis, Tennessee—Central Time Zone, 3 P.M.

126. Nebraska; Dodge City, Kansas

127. United States, Mexico, Guatemala; about 2,000 miles; about 1,000 miles

128. The second and third sentences are true. The first and the fourth can be rewritten as follows: Donner Pass was located on the California Trail. Santa Fe was located south of Soda Springs.

129. Students' answers could include the following: Georgia is bordered by Alabama, Tennessee, North Carolina, South Carolina, Florida, and the Atlantic Ocean. The capital of Georgia is Atlanta. Atlanta is about 500 miles southwest of Washington, D.C. From the physical map we can see there are three large rivers in Georgia: the Savannah which runs into the Atlantic Ocean, the Chattahoochee River and the Alabama River. It is also located north of 30° latitude and west of 80° longitude.

130. Quito, Ecuador: 0°; New Orleans, United States: 30°N; Porto Alegre, Brazil: 30°S. It is very warm because it is located on the Equator. Yes, because both cities are the same distance from the Equator.

131. Sacramento, California: 40°N latitude, 120°W longitude; Providence, Rhode Island: 40°N latitude, 70°W longitude; Honolulu, Hawaii: 20°N latitude, 160°W longitude

132. Richmond, Virginia; Kansas City, Kansas; Miami, Florida

133. Springfield, Illinois; 40°N latitude, 90°W longitude

134. Asunción, Paraguay; Antofagasta, Chile

135. Western Hemisphere; to check the accuracy of their clues, you may want to have students read their clues aloud and find one another's mystery hemispheres.

136. Mexico City, Mexico, and Caracas, Venezuela

137. About 300 miles long; longer; 150 miles

138. Columbus, Ohio; Norfolk, Virginia; Nashville, Tennessee

139. Madagascar; to check the accuracy of their clues, you may want to have students read their clues aloud and solve one another's riddles. Make sure geographic terms and latitude and longitude are included in clues.

140. The Mississippi River; Cities could include: St. Paul, Davenport, St. Louis, Memphis, and Baton Rouge; Answers could include the Central Plains, the Interior Plains, and the Gulf Coastal Plain.

141. Lake Mead; to check the accuracy of their clues, you may want to have students read their clues aloud and solve one another's riddles.

142. Norway, Poland, Turkey

143. Sierra Nevada; Sonora Desert; Death Valley, and the Great Basin

144. Harrisburg, Pennsylvania. Harrisburg is about 450 miles from Fort Wayne, Indiana, and Lincoln, Nebraska, is about 600 miles from Fort Wayne. You might suggest students use a ruler or map scale strip when determining distances.

145. Algeria, Mali, Mauritania, Morocco, Atlantic Ocean, Cuba, Gulf of Mexico, Mexico, Pacific Ocean, Taiwan, China, Myanmar, India, Bangladesh, India, Pakistan, Oman, United Arab Emirates, Saudi Arabia, Egypt, Libya, Algeria

146. Countries would include Spain, France, and Italy.

147. Little Rock, Arkansas; to check the accuracy of their clues, you may want to have students read their clues aloud and find one another's mystery cities.

148. Facts learned from the political map might include some of the following: Peru is bordered by Ecuador, Colombia, Brazil, Bolivia, and Chile; the capital of Peru is Lima; Callao is a city near the Pacific Ocean. Facts learned from the physical map might include some of the following: the Andes Mountains run through Peru; part of Peru is in the Amazon Basin.

149. Nigeria is located just north of the Equator–0° latitude and just east of the Prime Meridian–0° longitude. A traveler could sail across the Atlantic Ocean to the east coast of the African continent and then they could take various routes through such countries as Morocco, Algeria, Mali, and Niger, just to name a few. The countries that border Nigeria are Cameroon, Niger, and Benin.

150. United States; Vietnam, China, Mongolia, Russia